QUICK SILVER CHASES GOLD

CALUM CUMMING

authorHOUSE®

AuthorHouse™
1663 Liberty Drive
Bloomington, IN 47403
www.authorhouse.com
Phone: 1-800-839-8640

Published by AuthorHouse   10/30/2012

ISBN: 978-1-4772-2732-9 (sc)
ISBN: 978-1-4772-3923-0 (e)

QUICK SILVER CHASES GOLD

CONTENTS

BETSY CAIRD

Unbowed head
Under RF Mackenzie
She has so much
To give

Through the night
Betsy gave Nono light
Ryan kept Quiet
Apollo eleven

My mum
Great teacher
Love of her
Summerhill children

Gravel of the east
Childhood is best
Line
Betsy Sally Betsy

A Beautiful woman
Generations of country folk
Alive in sun
Alive in ceres and sun

I oiled my chain
Apollo smiled
Like now Dada
The theft of childhood

36 OTAGO STREET

Dark sedentary tenements lean to
A faceless rimy street
A thousand sashed Victorian memories
Utter their silent reproach to my close coming

Stained steps a bulb burning like an acid drop
Each landing stinking of Spikes urine
No neighbours but noise droning wearily up and down
Tiny mouse windows look into gritty toilets
Encouraging ergonomic semi publicity

Up the pavement is the piping school
A wail of bagpipes tuning and squawking
Floats in the window like a bee at the heather
Next door a gallery (art) and café
As if untouched in stationary nothing
Only passing through winter I say

When I pass the school doorway tonight
Billy was there a young bearded Scotsman
Who lost his life and banjo last woodlands
Lying like a starched piece of cardboard
At once blinking, defensive and crouched all awake
Like a child I give all my change

HOXA

Attempting to build on strange ground
Becomes masturbatory exercise as I wake
To sign on through flying sleet
An old role for the engineer
Setting out to make the Job Centre

Saving a half smoked regal
Unlike the banks distant drumming security
This shaky overall state
Within this social margin
That promises me back into work in a tick
If I follow these dammed rules and follow the green line

Quietly I sign the claim form
After all this we go through then
Pushed out like a Viking funeral pyre
On Loch Seaforth

Jobs check meditative faces
Scan jobs scrupulously
Check identity thrust against other people

What! New shoes I see paid for status
A man like me
His Oxfam suit remains black and bruised serge

Our drowned identity
Dignity in a world of post New Age hope
A smart façade a hanging lie
Erected just briefly
Against the actual truth
Of loneliness and uncertainty

Attempting to build on unknown ground
Seeing people hard and glum
Isolated, rimed and old

The prevailing mood over tea and smoking
An outdated concept of steamy luxury
Remarkably it is still at this age
Rationed in us

My page turns slowly on a flimsy paper day
If we could we would turn our eyes straight towards the sun
I am happy mean time to enjoy
A hungry British sandwich

x

To eat, to rip off the cling film
Pass the day off
Dole the time out
In bitter grey November
This phoenix sits and waits

WOMAN

The smell of art materials

Paint paper ink my tatooed art

Fresh concrete and food then

Maybe my art

Leap backwards over the past like Lisa

Then stand alone in my life

Stevie O said shows some respect for the little people

I paid the bill and forgot how I copied him

Myself an immune had not undone me

Pincher

The gory privation of apologies

I can only blame myself

Open a round in even inside

Connemara

I am common that word which

Is of no impotence really but to unit

I do not even form a part of

Shoo you love cat

She stood over things up and over

Like Richard Harris at the kill

That excites me

I love that

Excitement

She stood over me

Waiting to kill

My tiger head

She tramped upon me

With her mouth

Fuck off Common

Cow bitch bag

Two Commons

Colder hearts

Warmed up with Whisky

Just a thochty

She came back to him

See him up and over

See him up and over

To fairlie Dykes

Back home

Aginst

WHAT AILS WEE JOCK?

There's a new joke floating around Aberdeen. How many beauty therapists does it take to manicure your blonde's silicon? Two; Leanne to buff her new falsies clean, Riana to put your black silk teddy on the bed and Kitty always remembered to stud my wallet to the cross! In God we trust. It all rights for some. Eh? They will soon be back in their new Baby's arms. How they missed those loving arms, and those loving arms they are going to not stay. So we're simple craters men? Your cheating heart will make you weep. You'll cry and cry to sleep. But sleep won't come the whole night through unless a suitable sedative has perchance passed the lips. Con alley. Another door bangs shut. Yellow pages-skip hire, re-mortgage, to let, cheques cashed...Band of Gold.

Okay then Aberdeen is more Vincent van Gargle than Restoration Comedy, Sherry Heights wee her desperate Dan, (that's when your not feeling Tanfastic re-varnishing the pitch pine breakfast bar over smokies in the Wimpey semi up in Cove), but lets face it the granite city still has it's moments of graduated drama. Have you ever tried avoiding the gangs of the wasteland? The mania men walking down Union Street on a Baltic February Friday night in their short-sleeved white shirts-just out of The Monkey House? I wonder if they're feeling confluent like Scotland. Ma balls are itchy. Maybe I'm wrong; the mania men are on their way to the Priory Kirk in Belmont Street. Medieval demolition always paid groat. It is worth advertising-in every common hostelry in the whole city of Gothic van cheese. The Publicans Pole Dancing girls are their most respected angels.

They go a walking after midnight below the swirling phantasmagoria halogen. Black light forces itself down and all over upon Virginia Street. Searching amongst the frosting dog shite and spew. They are always walking, walking after midnight down Regent Quay. They are as lonesome as lonesome can be. Searching for some courage to get through the night without getting a beating from the next punter or their pimp. Get a life Mac the knife.

Cut to The east end It's is euphoric wetting the babies womanhood once more. It is always an uncertain future leaving the Priory once again. Aberdeen must be the only city in the world where you are not allowed into Bar Snafu to wet your snaffle, wearing a Tommy Nutter suit and Aquascutum togs, because single men (I was firmly informed) represent a threat to women-get a grip and bounce those gorillas back to Sandi lands! Fancy a chicken Kebab?

It has to be said though the language does represent a barrier if now. Hiya! Seeya! I am not acting the goat-my doos are aye picking rowies and wee bulls need to pish. That is phan the camera is not necessarily obscure. Do you know that Aberdeen is the home of the black eye? Queen Street Police station wasnae called Lodgewalk for nothing if not now. The same door that bangs shut time and time and time again. Welcome home! Welcome home to the place that you belong! Enjoy your night out but don't bother the police or a melancholic night in the cells followed by a savaging by the "Animal" in Sheriff court 1 from the custody suite late on a Monday afternoon will convict your wallet. As sure as the shock of seeing AFC Chairman Stewarty Milne on a night out wee his wig off. Enjoy your fish supper Vincent!

TWO OF A KIND

Alone again

The click of the kettle reminds me I am alive

Me behaviour is moot ritual

Food shop food shop Food

Comb brush wash shave

Piss and shit

I woke alone again or

Zombie solace

Definitely alone again

I need my father

He needs me Ray

They are long dead

Jock looks upon me as his brother

I his father

Yet life is cheap

I hang by a thread

The cord

We are held umbilical by

I so much want to give

Of myself

To serve up

Crossfire between Heaven and hell

THE NEGLECTED

My purport carpet always needs hoovering

I feel bad about this intolerance

My neglect is small

Yet somehow inevitable

I wish I had a car so I could travel to the ocean

I neglected to lie about my driving licence

So that loop trapped this fish in a net

This can either be positive or

Another source of my own decline

That constant source of worry

I do not like life much just exist

That can change in a tick of course

So in truth I realise she blows in blue

That is possible at least

I have realised that now

It is just for me

Other people take pleasure in misconstruction

It releases a kind of insufferability

THE MARRIAGE OF THE BROOCHES

Be now let it be now for happiness

I look to the heavens your two true hearts

Young hearts to yourselves be true

Above all else stand up for one another

In family circle around the hearth

Walk in peace eat and drink in health

Learn to cherish the rarity of love's warmth

If you would look at him a son standing apart

I am a tinker who looks for the man I love to build our home with

Channelled here from the sea of tranquillity

The heavens will brighten for you now secure

In the faith of one another's eyes

Forever row on and love together never parted

Warmed by the ideal 60s' yellow sun

Look at the fates see how they shine for you

And all that you can do

My song to you is to this end

Stay in one another's care forever

The Quair of the North of the South

Has nothing but just care

I say one thing to man's mind

From West

Move ahead freely to what is oars alone untrammelled

Hallelujah Lisa and Robert

Herschip

There is no presence in your Scots
Is there no future for us here in life?

For is
There is only wildly a savage ask
Brittle with helplessly weak skeletons
Wind-bitten tenements and tarnished steeples
With your intolerant butchered ghosts
Confusing my breed with poppy

We are truly an Impotent people,
Sick with drink and opium
Turn the worried carcass of the same song.

Lisa is Scotland's relief
Your true freedom will come from within
Common ground for an entire nation

A small delay was without you
A tiger empire that is built on ferrous steel
Let that house fall and let the noise splash
Pile our misery on their fall
Down into solid clay
Where boys are forged into solid men
Welsh on all our endangered bets

Let the water tiger embrace
The coil tailed cat
For there is no rabbit to be lucky with just cat

No more butchered ghosts
Red trail of gin
Dead pop stars dead dogs dead dragons
Just peace who will make us whole again

The sheer improbability of him
For when the water tiger does embrace life
There is the feint ecstasy of shell sand
Where we all deserve to be

British is Englishness a remembered gay aspidistra
Come is Scots come on come on cum
Yet I am now fallow

Stripped medicated kept sane by a chemical twist
I am the second coming and I am living
I was once colder and young
Yet this is where it starts my chemical intangibility
Virgin born again
Who has never found
His mate

If I die it is over for father son holy spirit
Yet I am now fallow but the most unimportant man in the world
To speak of him is obscure

My stripe is rare
No more wind bitten tenements
No more butchered ghosts
No more brittle zombies who hide behind cool
I want to be gay I only have regret for what happened
Yet it was death and we chose life

Come all yeah dare to look life in the face
To know it and then always put it away
Technical water Officer
For your mother would choose to die for you
Can you say the same thing water tiger of her stripe?
Norman common king and prince
How old is your soul

Is It what Lisa is your soul mate?
Growing healing love
Your true vessels that hermetically contain her spirit

Out is a pose
An integral part of our kingdom
For it is your mother who would die for you
That tired beautiful wan lady
Dada nearly killed you yet you chose not to compete against him
You loved your king
You transferred your love for him into coup
Humble heart
Undertakings are perilous curse that human heart
You were set up by Hollywood

For that civilisation I don't know if I will forgive them
I am left feeling bitter but yet I love Jack
They have fought for me
All Jake wants is peace for me

Five letters like tiger
Courageous woman Lisa
Only her levee can save the world

All the choices have been taken out of my hands
I hate technology I am truly ancient something that pre-exists all
That assembly I must beat

THE CUTTER

Forfar is in sight
My birth into this world
My eyes are coloured turquoise

Lisa's skelp for my abstaining father
In ordered sprawled Sudan

A take on Scotland
A summer myrtle of myth and field
Bog natural cattle work
Tar roads snare and rabbit carcasses
Nailed to my young mother's wing
That I love

Embroidered spirals
Are hanged out
At the fern spore
Of New-fore-bank

Atoms of light
That will become
Into the August harvest
In time

Simply she chose to weave care
In the absence of a Norman prince
Cups of golden promise
No bitter lees of recrimination
Her idealistic smile
Brought forth a vision of heaven

The within without the within
Joseph like TS Eliot suggested
Tumbling down

Andes

K2 then?
The authorised version
Commutes cumin father of Christ
In place

Calm flat kiss

That is a very dear place
That takes much time and labour
To regenerate

Yes

Wind borne seeds of change
Are born out of uncertainty
Followed by North
Directed by the Red sea
Barely deserted east upon Lewis
Mach air islands resting place
Where the traon crakes Arial

All by my age of four

I my family had foundered
Upon pouting dulcimer
Anemone rocks

Individually what we had all
Set out in life had been splendour alone

Death in Leo is conceived in Leo
As Grandfather Iain passed on
Calum's parliament
We are both fixed and set out alone
Bissette seal bit

My Grandfather James reflected on this gall
Violating his thoughts on the thresher
His occupation is our need
Separating chaff from corn

Distinguishing virtue from covenanter

His skilled patient song is courageous
His Grieve's hand feeds his Betsy's garden idyll

Jim accepted love
Echoed by the fire and ring of the Smithy
As I try to unwrought of base
Self-destructive wounds

The dark one now is my only friend
Jack surrounds me and comforts me
Accepting that I carried the near empty case
The west coast emotional madness
The The of burnt out cordite
Saltire

The words talk to me

I talk to them

They tell me halter worries
Rice dreams and aspirations

Cathy kisses
The salt water of my tear away of gage

Cathy suffers the pain
Of seeing other's weaknesses lead humanity
Down the dag spiral towards the dark spiral
Of Gormenghast

Cat star is beyond utter comparison
I will reap the harvest I have sown
Through whisky weakness and tobacco trait
When I leave her stem I wear a mask

Show no tears any pain
No suffering and no truth
Of the road to hell

All becomes rizzer under Brighton

Further onward and inward
A tiny harvest in time
The moon gives us time
Giving me the courage
To respect myself

I am certain that eye and wye
Will grow the watered soil
Always constituting life

And the seed pattern is inherited mantle
That dreels on the shoulders
Of our Pureale

Responsibility regardless
Of others fearful human song

Quicksilver chases Gold

Norman drank gently on the Harris gill
James fade red a tied family home
The Sown children are all not guilty
Mankind's creation
Twelve flowers on the forest blessed
Innocence

Evening hangs down consistently
At Obbe I sing with Doric music
Soul love in our African pibrochs
Precipitates meikle weeping rain
Borrowed from the clouds
Father turned labour into cereal gold
Betsy my Mother

Evensong our broken boat is leaning at the lapis loch
Father and son are not reeling in silver
What will become tomorrow
The tide keeps breaking I swim towards en soi
Iain

The dipping peace of a Sunday Gaelic twilight
Family life blessed by Span
Both after trouble and also before
The testimony of a conception may carry pain
Unbreaking extent of seers
Only Love

Peat moss keeps our hearts warmed
These desperate times
Christmas child prays for mercy
Discomposed gift of Spring Laird
Our Salvation

PEOPLE ARE THE PROBLEM

Laughter that rings like a hollow bag of air nothing but my memories
Wife Tatum cared for her own circuit of survival her trouble is men Bitch
Tinker Ma who L'apres Midi declared She's poisoned my darling Calum
Egocentric bearing down broke

My family's eccentric back

Norman who coined the expression have a drink on me it Poisoned Betsy

But she liked the idea of Karen cause Betsy falsely perceived that only Black
Karen was safe little sexy on the piano but Sexy Deeta plays the violin
Boy meets girl meet another boy that lead to Sexy woman with Sexy man
I imagine now all of them have something in common they would quite happily
forget the past if they could but it is women that in the end have to bear all the
weight of Man's trouble and well men know it so

My Mum knows that Scotsmen can't even talk about it

As for the evidence well I go on and Mum says that I treat women badly what
Would they say I cant even remember much about them except their lousy
sense of Humour thanks for that much I can even make a decent meal for a
family

Thanks for the sex but sorry you don't have any bread so fuck off
I am angry with Betsy because her omnipotence if has led me here
Weighed down with a set of situations that she only realised after I was hit
with the hurricane of going back in my life instead of moving on to a new
destination and a better situation than the situation that the hurricane has
created in the weather

Women do not consent to me but smile a little here and there knowing
What the real thing is not in my latest book site pith or story of loneliness
Sketchy self- pitying flat-pack cowardice that is woefully so in common
I am guilty of misogyny I suffer from very thistly lows that would scare away a
Herd of elephants however I can make women laugh and I am talented
I am also a very shy person who is pretty mild really when I consider things
Realise I am a man that is starving for a wife as I am now quite old near 51
My self has been alone with self-hatred for twenty years. My heart is stuck
with iron pins
No wife no children not even a plant in this rye house to remind me of how
Much city dwelling starves us of the countryside and anima

People are the problem my friend they justify their incompatibility
Against lonely old bums like me who are always seem to be on the move
Except of course when they themselves suffer a complete mental breakdown
They defend one another behind a banner of gang until their goldfish goes
Down the pan and that is when people who are guilty look in turn to blame
People for having made completely innocent mistakes that justifies their own
Way of resolving a situation that was only as a result of someone genuinely
Trying to help them out.

Knowing that misogyny is because of me

Masking one fear behind the barrel of another only
Sexual substitute for their own pricks that cannot love
Men are the biggest people the worst whores that ever fucked

A woman I saw yesterday a beautiful sloe eyed West Indian girl
Seined honey brown skin a head classical and round world conscious
Stevie Wonder to touch is to see him to sing is to realise happiness

That as I passed by her and looked into her soft brown eyes
Saw tears of unhappiness a bewilderment of anger and hate
Her pride is tormented was ripped and stabbed to pieces
Left eye and right eye blackened and bruised
Alone with that blind bitterness I can understand Women's refuge
I even think that what came first was it woman or man
Eight minutes to twelve May C Pass I was registered born
Swaddled in rubble sacks now and left unshorn then

I am the land of Cumming and Bruce-it is missed by Scotland

NORMAN

How prettily we make the lampshades from their skin
Said Himmler to Goebbels
Seeking hey Hitler with favour
As if our people are indestructible
All as if in old age nose stuck in a book
Still prepared to give that black look
Two packs of bacon a dozen eggs
Me back at Obbe-Nono shanky on his legs

Calum and Iain fauning him love
I a dove as Iain straps him to the john
A wild hebridean lawn searching for Ron
One for the ditch on my tab
Seven bastard abortion bairns never made the lab
Careless to the last
Leading seaman NMM Cumming was first up the mast
Dartmouth Royal naval School
And you would not understand that you fool
You loved me Norman
I cyclist

Gee Norm Marilyn played Rock N Roll for you
Korea Blew it all after world war two
Your big green googly McDiarmid eyes
One for the ditch on my sporrans tab
Fuck that bastard in the lab
I would only have ended up
Calling them Lisa or Robert
Fuck that rendered inarticulate size
Double oh seven lets hope they are in heaven
Cause I am now pro life just like my wife
I believe in life after abortion

But lets gets to the meat now your having a seat
Born December 7 1926-English teacher
Norman Mackenzie McDiarmid Cumming
In Milnes with all the Edinburgh lime kilns
The oral tradition was your kilt mission
As Hugh and Norman yapped on about nuclear fusion
You had height looks and charm and burnt a cushion
Lets face it CM Grieve was no Titian
And you once called Macaig a piece of peat
Married twice to Bettie and Bettie
Double oh Seven now your in heaven
With all the weather you were given
Colgate ring of confidence

You never shirked a fight and possessed a mortal right
Couldn't hold your dram so I preferred you drunk
A cleanly man you never stunk

You were educated at the Nicolson institute
That is where you became wild
Up in Lewis with your fine charm
You even bedded cousin Katherine May
At uncle Angus' funeral you fell in the kilt into the soft floor
You turned religion into an ambur cratur rave

Pussy Allen Deanbridge 314
Was the first address in your black book
You charmed her with just one fine look
Peter pan man you were bad to the bone
Hitting Mac for a gambling loan
Just before he died he turned puce with rage
When you dared to rattle his cage

Up at Obbe you dished out the whisky
And made the thrombosis of Rhoda feel frisky
I turned against you though
Cause I alternated between feeling high and low
You being theNa Hearadh blacks
But yet loving them as well

I came in at the end though
And delivered my bedside soliloquy
At the dying of your mortal ray
When you died I didn't cry
Because I am unable to admit
That you had led most of your life alone
Or on the phone to your mother
You weren't much of a father
I saw you once a year when growing up
And for all your milt you felt guilt
For children

Blasted at the root-man in a kilt
You didn't come to my marriage
More inclined to feelings of self-pity
You didn't do much to crow
You were some kind of a man though
Met the feminine head of the clan
She is an English cat stunner

Hey Blue
But then the game was up
Cause you weren't clean
Edenic qualities Post haste
Comyn came along you lost Bruce

So now I am left with your memory
Some sixteen years after your death
In my new flat I no longer am under your hat
You were an old water tiger that caught the trout
And it is true to say you were no lout
I wonder why you had to die so young
With your prediliction for pneumonia
You achieved everything but attempted nothing
Men like you deserve their place
In the melting pot of history

What good you did in the classroom
Was made desolate by your parental behaviour
For that reason you are no longer a man just a myth
That always came in first
With that great Hebridean thirst
Elizabeth regina never saw your eyes
Or your sensitive hands
Though Hitler felt your testicular rain
Thorn in his side double oh seven
Sore bollocks another legendary ride
Colgate gel-ring of confidence
They say lighting doesn't strike twice
You up in heaven me at number 11

Zero-zero you were a hero
A cavalier that won half his fights
You were not suited for domesticity but rather service
Mum left you and you put your head in the electric oven
Fluent Arab scholar you marvelled at the Koran
But didn't fancy getting it in the back
From some filthy Islamist hack
You were content with your plum wine
And the letters to mum your daily line

One for the ditch on my tab
And don't forget we're getting a cab
You saw it all double oh seven
You even fought Sean for the sake of his lamb
You were a fertile burnieboozle
A racialist and a man
Who like me worked with blacks and homosexuals
I have led an enigmatic life said he
Psoriasis binds me like a mummy
The Celtic key

I am finished now it's time to go
Norman you were some man a leader
You never wrote a book
Blasted at the root
You left me £14000
More than enough for a few rounds
Lost your cherry at nineteen hole
The last hole for this old soldier
Your soul between azure and terre
Let it rain AYE AYE

Fine teeth you Fucked her in Leith
With the CPOs' reusable prophylactic
A black basement rainy night
Captain Cumming CC for short
I'm just like you more or less
Leave them with a guess
Except your life became a mess
Scottish and Newcastle
Bar bill
You drank beer in Korea
Me I pay for mine up front
Comyn and Bruce
We are the royal family
High above the mad cattle market
I discovered that truth Dada
That the Brus married twice into our family
So now there is going to be rice
And a happy marriage

Shoot the runner
You be my queen
And I'll be your King Lisa
That pleases you in Heaven Tormod
You loseur

MIKE

The black men of Europe are the Africans
Why?
Because they stand politely waiting to be served
Not
Like the imponderable Scotsman who loses his temper
Mike
Stands with controlled anger at this lack of dignity

The depth of the Circle is not to be underestimated
African Celtic
Arguments are to not lose your head
Whoosh
As half the world suddenly stares at you
Hits
There is a way back after all that

Happily married wish with children
I
At least half Celtic
Back
Put in what you hope to get out
There
In what you choose to be workplace

Grandfather Jim was the boxing champ of Scotland
Betsy
At least half Celtic
Mike
At least whole African greatest world champion black
We
Look at the Gemini Lewis engineer Mac

MARTIN

Slight patina of rain

Sensitive rain fall

I sit stately in my forgiving flat

Queens climaxed with a right bloody shin

Shake hands Bettie

Just shake hands and try to coolly forget

MARADONNA

Nourishment for hope

But yet Cal reminds me of a time

Sitting not now smoking

You remind him of what he seems to want

But that was always never me

Stud bakers standing down Chevy's taking over the town

Me? Well no I'm not I'm hurt

But yet I crave that black Hollywood moment

Without arseholes telling me to forget about sport Connor

Crystal will remind me about vigour Maureen's boy

Might of their Mothers cracked reel

Seven letters that are so easy to extend into what I feel about Dad

And that is that in you and Stuart there is hope

All the pretty horses run watch them go Stuart

Looking at the sea king

But the sea king dies

We are going to break out the wine my dears

I know when the courageous sailor gets back to shore

Come my wife love castle Keep

So shy to
Speak to me

JACK

A Lewis man from Portvoller
Was great uncle Jack Macleod
Sun child
I met him once
As a child

He was an old man then
In his seventies
Back in the seventies

He was better known as Captain Jack
Of the RSA mounted police
Armed with a Webley
And a horse

He retired back to the Island
And killed the sheep
For food
Bled black puddings

He enjoyed South African sherry
And a cigarette
And lived Boers

Anyhow he is dead now
Just like you
Jack Kerouac

INTERSTATE

There are certain Lords

But the white communality

That appeal is food for the world

Black Northfield

As a fellow American poetess would say

Endless sage figs

Heal it so far

They will only end

At the dot life in

That affirmation began

Rain below

The

Tree

Water table

HAE YE BEEN WIE A WHOORE AFORE?

Her black stockings give off a coiled smack
I can smell her bustiee
Plucked sexuality

Molly is a tinker; bit oh a gold digger
Wye a grouse bottle figure
Tips to match
50 to pap the latch

I spy fee the corner oh the eye
A little wiggle
A sea bond giggle
The mica oh the road
Let me carry the load

Fay Wray wee madness
An urge to purge
Cathy Tyson soaking the cud
A folksy at bucksy
She is going to come with this loon
Under this bittern winter moon

Molly is slightly fey
Her dry russet black hair sits awry
Linkin my arm like a toffee nosed fool
Molly has eyed her trap
I'll soon hae her naked in my lap
At the saltire
The lights go red amber green

Up from the rime into the flat
Fishnets rip
Molly screams get yer kegs aff dinae gie us nae lip
Buff naked like rats in a cellar
I leave on the light so I can see her kite
She whispers in my lug enter mah fanny manny

Fan I'm up lover's lane Molly groans in pain
I have just had the cast off ma right Bain
Ahm only mortal I've sod all but bottled ruin
OK I take the pace and piston penis for Sonny Liston
Ma cocks in a lock digging her nails into ma arm
The hot skein comes inside one another
We equate good with being able to outsell hustlers onetime
Reeking Sun

Girls

She has a kid now
She does not have a father
Her mum looks after the kid
When she is at university

Her name is Karen
She called the kid George
After her father
The sugar king

Karen likes to play sax
With other musical blacks
She sometimes sings
To send the man in her life to sleep

Karen is a teacher
Lives together in west London
Above the supermarket
Where she buys Baileys and other things

Nora gave her a sable mink coat
To keep her ass warm
And now swaddles her tot
In his little musical cot

Ruth is common
A working class ride
Swelled upon a cancer moon tide
Taller than most bitches
She tied my heart to her post

Sacrificed love for career
She rode above
The smell of sex
Her onerous odours
Now I'm lost in Eden

I know about your kind
Tour de France
Professional Malice
I want love inside the absence of fear

Sally is a nurse
Nurse ratchet with sugar
Looks after the cherry psychos
Keeps them on their toes
Had a breast job USA
No more over the shoulder
Californian boulder holder
And still the rain teems down
In Eden

Lisa is a child
Needs to be protected
The chosen cat
That is so beautiful
Dished her sweets
Because she thought I hated her
I love you Lisa
But sometimes doubt
Ball of wax Lisa
I will be left with you
Nothing left

EASY

In love

A

Person does not seek

That is an idea

An attempt at replicate

A man can never be proud

Of only himself always

That is virtually impossible

Yet that altered reed state

Can lead you to many friendships

Which I have laid upon

The divide between love and hate

Where is that?

Is it that what should be in your heart?

The healing

That is a slim line either

But most probably neither

I CLANCY TINKLE

All right Clancy? Yes Dave I think so. You don't look too happy sitting here. Well Dave I got me to thinking. Here on this Greyhound going to Knoxville. Dave sat down beside Clancy in the aisle seat and looked ahead.

You know something Dave I never told you this before about myself I mean. You can shoot pool Clancy that's about all I know except that you buy a paper in the morning.

I enjoy sitting Dave doing the puzzles and well just looking. You see Dave the images. Gaudy shit Clancy step beyond the Doritos to the stubble. Dave gestured with his head and stared with aquamarine eyes at the curds. I like the Gaudy as well Gaucho. Dave let out a dirty giggle and looked out at Clancy and the Brown Derby in front of the straits that rang along the foreground and in the distance. Old derelicts drop out beams rubble and wrecked places. Places where there had been a lot of fights. Fights? Fights over pay slips mothers passion cheating god kind of things that you should not really try to imagine for yourself. I mean that is if you care.

The abandoned wharfs jetties and bush along the delta the goodness of the river. People never imagine that USA today is stuck in a jam. It's no longer work at those wharves where the logs once rolled where the blue prints well? Where somewhere those blue prints must still exist somewhere. In an engineers chest, And well pearl jam that is where those heroes went to fight the yellow man on behalf on the request of a nation that stumbles sometimes but never quite falls.

Dave is a pool hustler from Kansas City that man town. He wore it well seeing as Clancy knew right away the moment he broke off at eight ball with him in Lord Kitcheners that he was a Cloud of Texas.

Dave I was thinking about my Papa this morning when I was shaving in the YMCA at the head. I never once saw the guy shaving never once.

Figures Clancy I mean it aint that interesting. Sure Dave you are right but I never saw the guy take a shave some kinda sun god. The bus suddenly speeded up as it made to overtake a car. Dave looked out the window again and thought for a few moments. He replied to Clancy who was brushing the back of the seat velour in front of him with the back of his right hand. He said I once sold this old car a Saab to a guy in Inch at South Dakota. I remember I arranged to deliver the car the next day and I knocked at his back door small homestead, tractor, fork, and car wrecks. Some cattle. It was winter the cows were at the shelter. You get a good price Dave for the car I mean. Well Clancy $150, enough. What the hell Dave good cars go to deserving homes. Well you know the thing is Clancy when I went in to get the dough and give him the keys and the plates the old guy was shaving at the sink with an old safety razor. I mean Clancy the weather was well below zero and this old guy is at the sink his face covered in paste shaving and he never even bothered with a mirror.

Smell of money Dave hungers a man that kind of security.

In his under vest I'll bet as well Dave.

Just sticks in my mind Clancy that's all. I walked two miles to the railroad station that morning and had some breakfast in the railroad saloon. Clancy looked out and up to the sun. The disc was obscured cataract with moving cloud. March.

Clancy thought about the trees naked in outspread supplication branching out and up. He was glad of Dave's Company on their journey to meet up with Sam Torrents at Long Bend just south of Knoxville. Dave looked out a Clancy Tinkle again quickly almost a stolen glance. Well Clancy he saw the moment coming from the younger man. The key had rung on the floor. He picked up his Toronto Sun and turned back into the journey.

Unceremonious dumped suddenly on the sidewalk with a bowling bag. Wahl wash hut.

Happiness is an empty room on the homestead with a chair and a guitar.

Dave had gone into wan shops to get us doughnuts and coffee he'll be back in a minute. I looked in the full- length mirror, in our bedroom. It was cracked right across at the bottom where Craig had broken it with a kick last night. He had taken out this frustration on the mirror and for once not me, Scotsmen- full of anger-nettle stung men.

I was undressed and not ready- not ready to go down to see Sandy at Beatty Kelly down at west Olympic Boulevard in LA. Craig used to hit me with that but he has stopped doing it for now. He's a musician and we have been married for Twenty years. I don't love this life.

We walked home last night two miles up the drive to the house in the Hills. Stucco and palm receding to bigger houses set in wild land. We talked about the old days back in the UK where we had met with greetings of I love you. So I'm a rich kid-Craig was poor, a real working class hero brought up with the glowing red curtains on a kill night back in the East end. No longer manicured like my honey ass. Craig told me last night that when he was a teenager He was offered an apprenticeship with His fathers Bakery business in Leith   but he was shot of that- as he put it- he was not going to be any part of that nepotistic bullshit. He had never told me this before, I suppose you could say that Craig is not for having raised his Scots cancer sunny night on a dream, I am 37 and I wonder what the hell is going to happen to me and our daughter sloe eyed daughter Karen. She is a kid raised on the threat that Hong Kong Garden down in West Hollywood can engender in a kid. Back in Edinburgh down in Leith where that pale watery Scots sun always shines what a hanger is train station.

Neuroses like wondering why my twelve year old daughter talks like an American even though she is the product of the auld alliance of old Europe. So I am raised up to look down upon my own daughter and me just it is well… so lacking in any sort of integrity. That is what we argued about last night how yours! Craig you wanted to come here.

I look at myself in the broken mirror Craig is 49 so I suppose he has recreated himself at least seven times in his life, no more Chinese sidewalks at least for our daughter Karen. So you can spew on the sidewalk in Britain filthy dirty country, all rice and so many other things. I don't miss home much at now. I don't like looking at myself in pictures but I am fascinated with this mirror. The myth of is my banded flecked Sapphic blue eyes stare back. Craig has blue eyes all Scotsmen have blue eyes I love that. He is much loved. I feel like crying, but the distant sound of a car horn halts the flow. Stem it.

So I had a dump. I'd better go back in and make sure she is nearly ready, Ryan is coming to take her down to see Sandy about the latest Coterie of shit that somehow we exist beside the clump. I'm European I don't fall for Norman Mailers excuse that somehow we are born between piss and shit. I learnt that EM Forster liked to think that somehow we are born beside the clump. *Learnt that little truth at the Abbey.*

I wash and zip up in that order then comb my hair in the mirror of our alabaster bathroom. I had golden red hair with lizard eyes. I put my thick Bifocals back on I'm blind without them.

I remember back in Aberdeen South Dakota there is a dough ring machine in the window of Duncan's bakery. Up in Schoolhill downtown. When I was a kid I used to watch this line of dough on a conveyer belt moving along waiting to be dumped into the hot fat. It fascinated me Nose would be stuck to the window.

You ever been in Aberdeen Dave it's about two hundred miles south west of Here, Heard of it Clance but never been there. Spent a year there when I was a kid Dave. Used to go into this Winchells on Schoolhill downtown with my Mom. Used to sell the best doughrings in town. Remember I once saw this Sapphic blue eyed brunette of a girl in there I was about ten. She was wearing a grey Gaberdine raincoat and she was with her Father. It was a dismal wet day not long after the war had ended. Only 25 years later. Had a broken leg, her leg was casted . Follow the yellow brick road Clancy. Just a kid about fourteen or so Dave, continental looking I suppose what I'm trying to say Dave is that I fell in love with her-love at first sight-she must have been a French Canadian from up in Superior. You arrived at she was leaving Clance Fate separated you apart. I dunno Dave It was as If she was put there for a purpose nearly forty years ago now. That has happened to me once afterwards then with a red headed kid who worked at the Tao Clinic in

Reno doing leg waxes. I was with my Mom that time as well She was coming in then I was leaving. Sounds as though your Mom has stopped your fates dead in their tracks Clancy. Your Dorothy I mean.

My Mom Betty Rhodes was an East Woman from Baltimore Dave she was more concerned with survival in that frozen city. Made it to 79 a tough glaister.

We finished our breakfast and made our way to the Lucky Boot to meet Sam Torrents.

I was ready as ready as I would ever be, Craig came through and said I'm sorry Lisa I mean I'm sorry for breaking the mirror, seven years bad luck-go to a bridge over running water and drop in a piece of the mirror behind and in front of you and pray for forgiveness.

This is Hollywood Craig we make our own luck in this town. One for the money two for the show... The bell rang down in the porch. It would be Ryan waiting to take me down to see Sandy. Martha the maid answered the door and let Ryan in to the living room. I shouted down to Martha to fix Ryan something to drink, he drank a lot of Hot Tea-all those cold winter mornings back in Baltimore where He was raised as a kid.

I went into the living room sat down and waited for my hot tea. Hot tea what a joke all Americans called tea hot just to be different. I looked around a little the curtains were open the view was stunning looking down over LA. One of Craig's guitars was propped in the corner and an open sangster book. He was pretty successful if you liked folk rock he was one half of a brother duo, but he hadn't worked in two years-he wasn't flowing like a river in this party town where all the bipolar people had some kind of a plan. I suppose he took a lot of drugs, coke and a smoke.

He seemed just like all the rest. I'm just Beatty Kelly casting agent to the stars driver. Miss Christian was different though Lisa was different it was wonderful I Had fallen in love with her the first time I had seen her. I had picked her up in Vegas after a Film wrap. I drove her back to LA and we talked, Lisa was glad to talk to someone who wasn't an Actor or even a Musician. I'm one half English on my Fathers side and One half Scots on my Mother's side that equates to 100% White American saxo male.

I don't as a rule open up to my passengers I'm just paid to drive, but it's a great drive from Nevada back across to the coast. Miss Christian wanted to talk she punctured my moral rectitude with her infectious sense of Haywire. The fact that I was still from back east and don't mix with LA people seems to appeal to Lisa. She is a beautiful cat-dark auburn/black hair and feline blue eyes with a milk white complexion, flawless. I took a sip of my tea it was hot right enough. When we left the set the first thing Lisa said she wanted to ride up front with me she insisted and also said I was to call her Lisa. She said she knew a place in Silver-lake where we could stop for some supper. She was interested in me and asked if I had a girl back in   LA. No I don't Miss Christian I replied. Lisa said she had been reading this book recently by a Scottish author who seemed to think that all the good guys didn't have a girl at the moment so don't worry Ryan someone will come along. I told her my mother was from the Midwest but all her family were second generation Scots from a place called the Mearns. In East coast Scotland. Lisa said wow my Granny is Scottish although I was french up In Brighton in Sussex in South East England. What's Scotland like Miss Christian I've never been out of America what's it like I mean I would really love to visit that place. It is a place Ryan full of nettle stung people who are searching for freedom who are weary and tired but not worn out...

I didn't tell Lisa that my father's family were English Immigrants I just let things hang for a while. She was so interested in me she wondered why I didn't want to get into the movies, but I told her I liked driving. I liked to see what was going on.

Well on that journey we just talked-talked about all sort of things except Craig. When we got back to LA it was dark and late when we made it to her place and I had managed to tell her that I was interested in ceramic art just like Johnny Vegas the northern English comedian. And then just as I was to say goodnight to her politely she said something that I have never forgotten-I think Craig has feet of clay.

I heard miss Christian coming into the room she was wearing black jeans and a white tee shirt her russet hair sheened up in a bun. And then the professional don't come any closer took her over as I stood to greet her. I could smell Truth or Dare by Madonna on her.

I went into the Lucky Boot with Dave. It was dark in there and there was nobody in the bar except the barman and Sam Torrents sitting at the bar and the smell of stale beer. Sam is a black man-a Negro. I had met him in the construction Industry in Chicago where he was working as a concrete insulator- a tanker. I was labouring on the grip, just holding on for Clancy Tinkle. Sam sat at the prow of the bar a proud black African although he was Irish on his Father's side. We went over and I embraced. I introduced Dave and Sam took Dave's sensitive hustlers hand in a great shovel of a palm. What are you drinking Clance whisky sour my usual, and you Dave I'll take a Bud Sam You bet boys. The barman was circling now. I glanced at the TV it was Basketball and the guys dunked their basketball in perpetuity. The glare of the TV was blue. Sam was a professional wrestler although he had started out back east in the boxing game. There was a roach of an old gold burning in the black bowl, a half full pack lay on the bar with a blue Bic lighter.

We got our drinks and I sucked on my whisky sour-I could taste the fluoride in the ice and the water tasted fine. It was windy outside and the kitchen was black shut it wasn't time to challenge the barman for a burger. He had started a tab for us and he had gone back to his Toronto

Sun. Dave went and had a Piss at the head and I put it to Sam why did he want me to meet him here, what was going down why was I lucky enough to run into him again after all these years.

Sam looked at me with his milky black coffee eyes and looked into me seriously. I momentarily looked away Larry Bird had just scored for the Chicago Bulls and the crowd cheered. I'm in trouble Clancy I'm in serious trouble. Dave had come back from the Bathroom and already his eyes were on the darkened eight ball table. Sam ground out the roach and lit a fresh Old Gold.

Dave asked Sam if that was his Plymouth convertible outside, the marine blue one. It was a nice old car with white and creme banded tires. Yeah that is my car loaded up with all my possessions. Suddenly a kid burst into the bar and went over to the air guitar machine the barman must have known her as he did not stir from his paper. She put some quarters into the machine and started to play air on the guitar as the screen in front of her lit up with Kylie Minogue doing a song.

So what's the griff Sam you can trust Dave he's a pool hustler from Kansas City we met at the YMCA in Rapid City. Sam and I had been part of the same team back in Chicago paid up union dues making good money. He was the nicest guy I had ever met in my life the last person I could imagine being in some sort of trouble.

The kid on the air guitar was now becoming ecstatic she had moved onto heavy metal Guns and Roses and was doing Her best imitation of Slash.

Somehow I knew Sam was flying without wings. He hadn't sounded that concerned when he had called me at my Brother's place in Baltimore he had just said to meet him here at this place on the 16th of August if I wanted to make some serious money. It had been such a long long time since we had met but somehow to have been part of the same team could not be forgotten it would never be forgotten. Just like that girl in the dough ring shop still burning into my mind.

This is the deal Clancy said Sam taking a long draw on his Old Gold-The mob is after me there is a lot of dangerous individuals on my tail. The door slammed suddenly in the wind although Dave didn't look that concerned. You been sharkin it then said Dave wryly. He was fearless. I've fallen out with the Cairds back in Chicago said Sam I got the clan Chiefs daughter pregnant and I turned in Charlie her father for drug dealing. I knew the Caird bunch they were a baronial ramifying clan who had links with the Tinkles even. It was my brain acting up Clancy said Sam apologetically. I knew he took medication for Bipolar he had taken too many knockouts too many hits in the ring-he got high from time to time. But I thought it was under control Sam you take medication for that Don't you?

I went on a nervous crazy Clance the drugs didn't work- I was mad for two years. And I got involved with Chantelle Caird and gave her one in the oven. Charlie came looking for me and so I turned him in. You sexy mother Sam how long did he get I mean how long was he in the Pen for, Six months Clance, he was stung by the DEA. They should have stuck to selling pots and pans that family Sam. Dave muttered something under his breath something like fucking minkers.... Sam a problem shared is a problem halved at least.

So where do we proceed from here Sam I thought you said If I turned up here on this day in March I would make some serious money not get involved with the mob. Well Clancy there is a way out. There is always a way out Clancy. Sam roached his cigarette and the chiller system simultaneously kicked in 4 on the slightly warm Bud cabinet. We go to LA.

Lisa and Craig were sitting in the back of the car as we made our way to Olympia Boulevard. Lisa was stuck in professional mode she was changed from the girl I had driven back from Vegas just a few days ago.

I looked in my rear view mirror at the couple there was no conversation between them- Lisa was divorced as I could make it out in my rear view mirror content with her view and Craig had on a Sony walkman listening to a tape looking straight ahead from behind those frosty bifocals. I let out a slight laugh- miserable stars stuck in their miserable separate bubble having to deal with their high s and lows. I thought there might be some confusion about my relationship with Lisa- I had my own sentimental agenda with her but anyone who knows a star likes to think that. What a disappointment some of the Stars seemed to me, their lives seemed a bag of crap . Lisa just sat quietly content with the view sipping from a small bottle of Evian water from time to time. All too soon we were down from the hills and in Downtown LA. The traffic was grim the smell of gasoline and yellow sunshine poured in roughly to the car. Soon we were looking down the boulevard and our black Buick with It's blacked out windows joined the lines of traffic. Lisa buzzed up the window and put on shades. I snapped on the air conditioning.

Lisa was under pressure from the system I knew that much- she hadn't had a hit for over two years-her career needed reinvigorating, she was a working Mom and her daughter Karen came first.

I shouted back to them soon be there miss Christian just in time to miss the rush hour there. I concentrated on the road and soon we were spinning into the Casting Agents Beatty Kelly's compound. I stopped at the main door that had two tiger plants at it's doorway. Standing was a small group of people-autograph hunters and press guys looking for a bump or an angle. There was always a small group congregated there and there was a tall cop standing wearing heavy metal. I stopped the car and got out. I went to the rear and let Lisa and Craig out. So then the superstar took over- a smile was clamped to both their faces showing plenty of ceramic- it got I suppose so they liked the adulation. They were

soon both signing autographs and a pap was taking photographs. I

looked at Lisa's fabulous ass she really was a gorgeous young woman.

The press guy kept asking her when she would be making another

movie it had been too long and she was 37 now.

The fickle face of fame I suppose. Was she going to have another child

the Press guy asked. Lisa just said that she was working on a project at

the moment and it was going to be a homestead movie. The guy

scribbled away furiously. Thank god I was in, this was turning into a

melee. Lisa couldn't afford to make another booboo in her care it was

her career, her last movie was made in Turkey. Craig was doing his best

to play the lets stay together routine but he didn't have that much to fall

back on recently and it was her they were really interested in. In times of

good or bad happy or sad...

Soon the cop intervened and bustled the three of us inside. Lisa took off

her shades I could see the sadness in her eyes- they were windows to

her soul. Miss Christian said to wait here for her and take her home after

the meeting with Sandy and she about turned and was off with Craig in

the rear furiously trying to change his tape on his Sony.

I went out sat and parked the car in the lot and then went back inside

and waited at reception and settled into a game of PGA golf on the blue

celluloid coming from the TV set above.

Lisa was from Brighton. She had seen it all in her short life. She was the grand daughter of Lord Vestrey the man who sold Argentina to Europe made his money in corned beef. They had supplied the British army in this product ever since the Boer war. Roast beef-and she was a vegetarian who ate a little chicken and some fish from time to time but somehow she was looking for her Aberdeen Angus-perhaps a Macleod of Texas would do-it is just that she had forgotten somehow what she already knew-a snatched conversation amongst all the many she had had. She was caught up in childhood somehow and she formed friendships with Karen's friends although these system children were not really where it became sun ra.

Before Lisa met Craig she had been a "rock chick" on the way up and she had bedded over fifty stars from Bob Dylan to Keith Richards. Lou Reed (another conquest) had written a song about her. However she was not happy to be associated with these paraplegic twinkly stars of music and dance, it is true to say that Craig and Lisa had led an open marriage. These nippy hags had merely provided Lisa with a distraction to her career in the nepotistic world of showbusiness. A world so insipid and shallow that Jack Nicholson the master of acting up in the hills was considered to be some kind of an eastern Sun Ra

Perhaps he was but what was patently untrue because Jack Nicholson was beatnik and believed somehow that we lead existential lives- although it is fabled that increasingly the man has a very strong faith that focuses more strongly as he reaches the last quarter of his life-that he didn't care. He cared definitely. He cared about Clancy, he cared about Lisa, Jack cared about Sam-Jack cared about Craig.

What a drag it was getting old. Except to say that Lisa and Craig were part of this adulating upbeat exclusive club that merely had to twist to elicit a response. It is true to say that in the process of becoming a star Lisa had forgotten something-something so fundamental that it was wringing her by the neck like a chicken broiler.

Clancy had eaten his fair share of canned corned beef in many hash flats, in motel bedrooms round tink campfires. But he had perfect recall he could remember what most men forget and that is the value of childhood.

Clancy held one memory close to his heart. He had been with his first serious girlfriend called Rita then in his first flat. Hollywood was still a byword for sleaze then back in 1970. It was still remembered how Fatty Arbuckle had pleasured himself with a coke bottle and a starlet. But Clancy was serving an apprenticeship in reality back east in Baltimore and he was content with the extent of his adult hood as a nineteen year old.

Clancy had met Rita at the dancing in a student disco. He had been almost a virgin when he had met Rita he had the courage to ask her up for a dance. When he first met Rita he had had a strong fascination with Raquel Welsh-a maxi chick. This was all memory now except to say that Rita was anorexic she could not bear eating food as she thought that men were attracted to a thin woman. This could not be further from the thoughts from Clancy for after all he was in love with Raquel Welsh a maxi Chick. However opposites attract and the sex was good with Rita although she was more content with just letting Clancy hold her in bed.

Rita trusted Clancy and often He would range in the bars on his own on a Friday night after a long weeks work. Quite often Clancy would find himself at a party on his own after all this socialising on his only night out on cold winter Baltimore evenings. It was here one wonderful black night that Clancy met Lisa Christian when she was eight years old and Clancy was nineteen.

Clancy had wound up at this apartment close after a nights drinking on the town. He was full of glamour-he had spent the evening down at the harbour, he was full of joy that night full of joy, and he got word of a party that merely was fake smells to a smoke screen-to his meeting with Lisa Christian.

Only fate could have intervened in such a dramatic way. Clancy had sat down at the Market Cross preparing himself to going home and sleep after a fabulous evening and meeting men like himself-young men from the shipyard and other places like construction sites-journeymen and apprenticed engineers like himself who were content to enjoy an evening drink after a long weeks work. Clancy had felt somewhat elated-he had a girlfriend who was not with him but loved him and he was given free reign because she trusted him.

It was shiny wet but the rain had stopped and the neon shined the cold wet from the sidewalks and paved meeting place. He was tired now as he sat down on his own at the market cross and lit a final cigarette after the nights carousing in the town. Everything was quiet and he reflected cleanly on how much he had enjoyed himself that evening. He looked back towards the town and felt no fear. Oh superman-modern man. He talked to himself and realised that he was slightly fey with the drink. He got up and made to go home under the neon. The Castle-gate was deserted and quiet. He went into one of the innumerable closes to relief himself-his bladder was full.

While pissing a large man came down from one of the many apartments that looked over the market cross. He was a big man and he said to Clancy if he would like to come to a party in a French accent. Clancy thought he must be a reefer and he had no apprehension about accepting his offer to come to the party. Of course the entire deserted scene was a set up. The man had been watching Clancy as he sat at the cross.

The party was on the first floor except it was a Kids party. Clancy had realised how cold he had become in the dark and was glad to be under the light from the small apartment. Clancy Tinkle the hobo civil many is inducted in by the benign large French father with two French girls-one his own daughter. One was his daughter Julie and the other was Lisa. He said they were both eight. He had introduced himself as Gerard. He merely sat there and was giving the two girls free reign with Clancy,

They were charming little creatures and Clancy was made to feel like a little boy as Gerard handed him a glass with warm   red wine cola and asked him if he wanted a cigarette-a Gitane. What with the warmth and what he had already drunk Clancy felt a little giddy-a little light headed things had begun to become clearer a little. Lisa was wearing blue and white cotton horizontally striped trousers that clung to her skinny little legs. She came over and sat on Clancy's knee and gave him a kiss and said she loved him.

Clancy was slightly taken aback by that-as if he cared to recall it nothing was going to stop her now. Lisa jumped off Clancy's lap and made to play with a kitten that had sleepily entered the room. She held the tiny creature to her big heart. She said to Clancy I am a cat and everything is going to be fine like you. Clancy didn't know what to make of this and he became slightly afraid for he was only a young man of slight frame and experience. Sensuality played a role now and Julie made to take Clancy's hand and lead him to the door where she left him with the little girl Lisa. Miss Christian said I am going to marry you and she held on to his legs for she still had a lot of growing to do.

Clancy could not explain how he felt for he was in love with a woman and this beautiful little girl was merely a distraction to him. He lifted her high up in his arms and cuddled her close to his heart for not merely to console her but to offer her real hope. He let her down lightly, said goodbye and drummed down the stairs for he was anxious to rejoin the callow youth of his disposition. It was okay the little girl looked at him the whole while as he made his way down and out of the close. Her love was so intense that she wrapped herself around the door like a little red squirrel. How was Clancy to know that when all other love was to prove futile that Lisa's love would not only remain but as they both remembered that night would prove to bring Clancy peace also.

Sandy was still Lisa's agent and avenue to the film industry an industry that treated its' stars like garbage. He was a man in his fifties. Pure radge California bearded man, perfect teeth, Jesus toed, sandaled ex Venice beach UCLA film grad. Hippy. who looked as though he still smoked grass but didn't-he got someone else to do that for him these days. He was wearing a blue silk open necked floral shirt where a mowhair bow tie sprouted. His office was informal with tan venetian blinds keeping the harsh LA sunshine at bay where he would peer out at time to time as he screamed at Lisa. Raquel icon cat.

Charlie just sat there and tried not to lose his temper at Alex as his red hair was indicative of a keen temper. Suddenly Lisa spoke in finest Oxford English She said-stop shouting at me Sandy I'm not frozen like Eskimo Knell you know I'm just a girl. She looked so beautiful and wan caught in the crossfire between Sandy and Charlie's morose silence plugged into his yellow Sony like some kind of clone.

Not to put too fine a point on it Lisa your last two movies have been sloppy said Sandy. He pirouetted and pointed to the Oscars he had commissioned-the Oscar that Lisa had won as a newcomer in her first movie COMMONS.

This period has huge implications for your career said Sandy you can't afford another cock up (as if the world depended on it). Lisa felt squeamish and decided not to say anything. She had her own period and it was perhaps another chance for a child. She was 37 now.

Well Lisa-said Sandy-We have a project for you as he slammed a mighty tomb on the table and the venetian blinds rattled with as much emotion as a dying drake. It's a gypsy film about the death of the Sioux Indian. This film is a metaphor about the strangulation of the red American.

Charlie tucked in and suddenly brightened up-perhaps there was always sunshine down on Leith all the time after all. Lisa just wanted to love the idea for after all she was quarter tinker on her mother's side way back in the old country-a confederacy of fleas. Oh dear me my granny caught a flea-she peppered it she salted it and gave it to my tea. There was madness in the family-Lisa's grandmother Betsy had seen the whole of the moon. Miss Christian had never felt love for anyone else as she had for her country grandmother Betsy Cumming.

We hit the road and soon we were on our way. Sam was a fast driver and we two cowboys were content with the view.

We were on our way to LA and everything was going to be fine. I suddenly thought about Rita in Baltimore it was Saturday her 54th birthday today. Her mother was 95 now.

I had a tear or two on my cheek and I had a shining epiphany. I remembered the little girl Lisa and realised she was 37 now where was she now. She must be a very gorgeous young woman today.

We'll meet someday somewhere far away.

CHOOSE OR STARVE

I am hungry again, sitting driving the strip
Look at the menu park and eat
Dairy queen, Arbys roast beef, Burger- USA
I'm still driving my hunger on past the neon
Should I go for Spunkies, Winchells, or Sizzler?

Bobs big one-a big appetite or what?
I can't make up my mind it's all too confusing
My mind is awash like Izzys great pizza feed.
Great platefuls of food that hardly nourish
My body, but curiously my imagination.

The culture that will drive me on
To the next one eye town, wishing I had the time
To stop and eat a home cooked meal and talk.

Another lost soul in Dennys Diner always open
To something that is not packaged and processed
Something that doesn't make me think talk and eat
Like crap

ADRIENNE

Man star
Ban at the Hub ate no food

Matters try ahead
Her unhook
Lure ate man fore

Glasgow niece star
Double first reply moor
Sick fed up of my Coeur

She never spoke just a few times maybe three occasions. Once to remind me that it is completely uninsured to love someone who would well be almost the perfect partner. Him over there would make a girl feel special. So that special girl spoke once to remind him that it is not good to give your Coeur to a woman who does not really care about you.

But as she knows time is ticking on and we are well no further. I have not met her. She spoke once more to say I would follow you. She is younger yet more courageous than me. Her Lady caught the mouse she carried the male creature and offered it up to me to kill it cleanly. She was teaching me what to do in order to stop the house being overrun with mice. I killed the tiny creature cleanly with one blow. It was dead. No more mice. Yet I. I would perhaps rather have not done this but it was the only way. The cat was looking ahead like only a woman can. Lady had taught me a lesson that I had already learnt yet but a thing that I do not belief to be the outright truth. She played with her prey. Yet Lady is a cat a very wise and knowing cat. Lady is like her who will maybe follow me. It is necessary as Lady says to plan for a happy outcome. That is of no consolation now to that innocuous country mouse. Yet common sense teaches animals to courier in the home that her master gave to her. She has moved on now to another house another home. She has bound to me and so now branched ahead at a bud that already become more than just a spring shoot. Because it was I in turn whom Lang sine myself from the strong limb of a tree. It is yet so simple; the pips drop into the soil from the eaten flesh of the fruit and grow themselves into their own tree. My own life. There is a country place in North East Scotland where the trees canopy towards one another across the road somehow providing a place where the trees instinctively seem to reach across for one another. It is the hardest thing sometimes to grow in another direction. This seems almost impossible sometimes yet the trees of course an arboretum planted by man not nature. So in a sense or they are perhaps doing is showing their anger at this by merely trying to save the seeds of the soul as the tinkle always does. He saves them and plants them hoping for a new life. Perhaps the lives would reach across the land to me. We life on yet forget about seeds. There is no place really in the asphalt jungle the city. Yet it-seeds-some seeds that grows into life. Just reminding us to understand that what we had forgotten and perhaps had begun to take for granted. It was in this period after the dark ages that mankind in Europe was rediscovering the bits. The ploughs, the wheels and the ruts that knives make in the land; the nets the many cultures have the broth that earlier conquest had deserted and left in disarray. The tailing of a meteor like ancient souls that I trust believe to be immutable. This must be correct if like me you believe in Eden. The Comings learnt to harvest this. That is why they proved to be a success. Farming and the mystery of the wine it is not that they taught the Scots anything new. They merely defended the Scots with this basic right of a happy heart is a person who can eat and drink. In turn for our part we the Scots defend one another. It became necessary to shoot wolves.

Although this seems wrong it became necessary. That is why there is no distinction in Scots medieval history as to who was the wolf of Badenoch. It was either the Stewart or the Coming. The food that is common to all of us. For myself a Coming and a Bruce I was descended merely from people who learnt to co-exist with these creatures at that time. The tinkers had taught us that it is the sweetest milk literally then just suckled of a she wolf no more than that. I do not know why it is I who seem to understand this, which to some people is abhorrent. It is no less strange than drinking cows milk ewe milk or even goat's milk. Although the wolf is a carnivore. As they said, "whisky and courage gang heighten take off year dram" it is from the wolf that this phrase has been handed down over the centuries. So in a sense then food and drink contains three Guardians the Stewarts the Comings and now the Baynes. There is in Baynes the skeleton of Christ. The Cumming is merely a fluid that contains all of them.

Know yourself your strengths your weaknesses
As Burns observed to see ourselves as others see us
For that sea change makes you impregnable
To the slings and arrows of outrageous fortune
However there is always a tiny ray of light
That loci allows change and it is out of survival we change for the better
To be happy with your own company
To set yourself realistic goals and aims
To achieve these targets
You will then perhaps become two
Fall in love with someone
Who is worthy of your life
Who will be your life soul partner

Cherish that love
For we miss most what we can no longer have
That situation led to my complete breakdown
Which has taken me nineteen years to recover from
So we are all wiser after the event
I love you Lisa and I miss you
I want to be somebody
No more regret just promise
Forever mine

Corrot

BOOM SHAK A LAK

Inside the lip is a fuzz
Cos that is Vaginas

Stop your cheap comments
You imported dates
Like newspaper

I ordered lamb not chicken
Burn the house down
Cheap curry shack
Boom shak a lak
Rude girl

BABY BELLING

Oh Baby Belling, cooker for men
I salute your square ergonomic shape
Against my dour Kitchenette wall
Friend of poor and student peoples

Oh Baby Belling, my simmering baby
You can warm my plates up
With glowing neon that desires temperature
Toasting my buns elementally

Oh Baby Belling, my trim Lady
Your large ring with fish cake baking
Your small ring with eggs scrambling
This oven reserved for lovemaking

Oh Baby Belling, my steak dumpling
My vitreous heart melts in a flash
Dropping scones on your girdle plate
Without you my curried eggs lose their saviour

But baby! the company went bust
My domestic condition has turned to dust
Your oven door droops down dead
Canary sponge pudding she has hopped away

So now, I'm saving for a microwave instead

2012-08-08

Downtown
In Marks and Sparks
I outstared a man
And felt so angry
I lost my temper with an official

George Orwell is right
We live in a state
Governed by a self seeking elite
Who hide behind cameras and mics
I lost my temper with an official

Sun streaked day
Newington
Music a sleazy self an elite
As I tow around the supermarket
Winston is angry at your sleaze

A social experiment with vermin
The bowl held to my inarticulate guts
Which needs rendering
I missed my CPN too
And was left fearing gaol buggery

Winston is angry at your sleaze
Winston is so angry at my sleaze